WOULD YOU RATHER...?

Know what boys are thinking all the time

OR be able to make them say anything that you want?

Over 300 fiercely fascinating questions

to ask your friends!!

Courtney Bulestier

SUPER SECRETS!

have a teacher that teaches in rap OR Pig Latin?

Read your text messages aloud in class

read your diary aloud in class?

Not be able to keep a secret

OR not be able to tell a lie?

Edited by Justin Heimberg & David Gomberg

Published by Seven Footer Press
247 W 30th, 11th FL
New York, NY 10001

First Printing, July 2010
10 9 8 7 6 5 4 3 2
Manufactured in Baltimore, Maryland, July 2010
© Copyright Justin Heimberg and David Gomberg, 2010
All Rights Reserved

Would You Rather...?® is a registered trademark used under license
from Falls Media LLC, an Imagination company.

Cover Design by Junko Miyakoshi
Design by Thomas Schirtz

ISBN 978-1-934734-69-8

www.sevenfooterpress.com

Tough Choices

Adults always say you have it easy. Free shelter, simple schedule, nothing to worry about except history tests and whether you want that Frappucino plain or with whipped cream. But being a girl is hard.

You might not be paying a mortgage or working a full-time job, but you still face tough decisions every day: Would you rather have a crush on the school's star athlete or the valedictorian? Would you rather have ten casual friends or one BFF? Can I really pull off shiny leggings?

You have just as many choices to make as your grown-ups do, and the constant drama of school can make each decision feel more important than the one before it. So what's a girl to do? Well, start with the choices on the following pages. If you can handle those, then you're probably in pretty good shape. And just remember, no matter what anyone says, boys will always be hard to figure out.

Table of Contents

CHAPTER 1

Boys

Boys. Life would be so much easier without them. Then again, what would there be to obsess about? From swoon-worthy to barf-worthy, boys are a fact of life. As if you're not thinking about boys too much already, here are some boy-related quandaries to consider.

Would you rather...

sit next to a guy who has really long nose hair

OR

horrendous body odor?

Would you rather...

have the hot-but-jerky captain of the football team like you

OR

the nerdy-but-nice captain of the chess team?

YOU MUST CHOOSE!

Would you rather your crush have...

short hair **OR** shaggy hair?

blue eyes **OR** brown eyes?

money **OR** looks?

YOU MUST CHOOSE!

Would you rather your crush have...

contacts **OR** glasses?

bad breath **OR** bad manners?

acne **OR** braces?

Follow-up: What does your biggest crush look like?

YOU MUST CHOOSE!

Would you rather...

burp while a boy you like is talking to you

OR

have Dorito breath while a boy you like is talking to you?

Would you rather spend the day with...

Cole Sprouse **OR** Dylan Sprouse?

Adam Sandler **OR** Will Smith?

Jesse McCartney **OR** Michael Phelps?

YOU MUST CHOOSE!

Would you rather...

have a magical power that made guys turn bright purple every time they lied

OR

a power that made them slap themselves in the face every time they said something mean?

YOU MUST CHOOSE!

Would you rather go to a school...

that was all girls

OR

where you were the only girl?

Would you rather...

run into your crush while at the movies with your parents

OR

run into your crush with a major zit on your nose?

YOU MUST CHOOSE!

Would you rather...

spend the day with a boy who's too shy to talk

OR

one who won't shut up?

Would you rather...

have your crush like you for your personality

OR

your looks?

YOU MUST CHOOSE!

Would you rather...

have a bad case of the hiccups when finally getting to talk to a guy you like

OR

have a bad zit outbreak?

Would you rather...

know what boys are thinking all the time

OR

be able to make them say anything that you want?

YOU MUST CHOOSE!

Would you rather...

every time you see your crush, suddenly burst into song like in a musical

OR

shoot steam out of your ears like in a cartoon?

YOU MUST CHOOSE!

Would you rather...

someday marry a tall, average-looking guy

OR

someone who looks like Orlando Bloom,
but two feet shorter?

Would you rather...

have a reputation as a heavy sweater

OR

someone with severe dandruff?

YOU MUST CHOOSE!

Would you rather...

the boy you like best call you once a month

OR

literally, every five minutes?

Would you rather...

your crush catch you picking your nose

OR

farting?

YOU MUST CHOOSE!

Would you rather...

spend the day with a guy who was
dumb but hot **OR** smart but ugly?

super interesting but with terrible BO
OR incredibly boring but the most popular boy
in school?

someone who constantly makes you laugh but your
friends hate **OR** someone who bores you but your
friends love?

Boys

YOU MUST CHOOSE!

Would you rather...

see your crush flirt with your best friend

OR

your sister?

Would you rather...

spend a day with a cute guy but not be able to say one word

OR

spend the day with an average-looking guy and be able to talk as much as you want?

YOU MUST CHOOSE!

Would you rather...

study with a guy who compulsively picked his nose

OR

who took pride in belching the alphabet?

Would you rather...

your crush be able to sing like Justin Timberlake

OR

dance like him?

YOU MUST CHOOSE!

Would you rather...

join a study group with a guy who thought he knew everything but really didn't

OR

with a guy who didn't talk at all?

Would you rather...

dance with a guy who wore leopard-print shirts

OR

who wore socks and sandals?

YOU MUST CHOOSE!

While chatting up a guy as you're walking to class, would you rather...

fall down

OR

throw up?

YOU MUST CHOOSE!

Would you rather...

sprout a face full of zits during the day
of a school dance

OR

have explosive diarrhea that lasts 20 minutes
during the school dance?

Would you rather...

be asked to a movie via an ad in the school paper

OR

via the school loudspeaker?

YOU MUST CHOOSE!

Would you rather...

text your true feelings about your crush to—whoops!—the boy you have a crush on

OR

to your mom?

Would you rather...

dance with a guy who is 15 pounds skinnier than you

OR

5 inches shorter than you?

YOU MUST CHOOSE!

Would you rather...

a boy try to win your affection by writing you a song

OR

by painting a picture of you?

Follow-up: What's the most nicest thing anyone ever did for you?

YOU MUST CHOOSE!

Would you rather...

go to a dance with your school's star athlete

OR

the valedictorian?

Would you rather...

have five ordinary guys like you

OR

just one really special guy?

YOU MUST CHOOSE!

Would you rather...

have the ability to direct the movements of boys in your school by using a Nintendo Wii controller

OR

have all the fortunes you get in your fortune cookies become true?

YOU MUST CHOOSE!

Would you...

not speak for a week for the chance to meet Zac Efron?

change your name to "Lumpkins" for a chance to spend time alone with your crush?

ever ask a guy you like to dance?

always wear a sombrero if it meant you could read boys' minds?

YOU MUST CHOOSE!

Would you rather your best guy friend be...

Troy **OR** Chad?

Zack **OR** Cody?

Phineas **OR** Ferb?

YOU MUST CHOOSE!

Would you rather...

be rich

OR

famous?

Would you rather...

be famous for your looks

OR

for your accomplishments?

YOU MUST CHOOSE!

CHAPTER

Celebrities and Pop Culture

The life of a celebrity is full of difficult choices. Drive the Porsche or the Escalade? Buy a diamond necklace or a yacht? Live in New York City or Hollywood? Luckily, we ordinary people can just take it easy and watch from the sidelines. Still, it's fun to imagine...

Would you rather...

have Miley Cyrus's voice

OR

her bank account?

Would you rather...

be a character on *iCarly*

OR

on *Zoey 101*?

YOU MUST CHOOSE!

If there were a movie made about your life, would you rather it star...

Miranda Cosgrove

OR

Selena Gomez?

Follow-up: If you could choose anyone, who would you want cast as you?

YOU MUST CHOOSE!

Would you rather...

compete with Danielle Deleasa for Kevin Jonas

OR

compete with Ashlee Simpson for Fall Out Boy's Pete Wentz?

Would you rather...

swap mothers with Lindsay Lohan

OR

swap fathers with Jessica Simpson?

YOU MUST CHOOSE!

Would you rather...

be interviewed by Oprah

OR

Tyra Banks?

YOU MUST CHOOSE!

Who would you rather have lunch with?

Prince William **OR** Prince Harry?

Shia LeBeouf **OR** Johnny Depp?

Robert Pattinson **OR** Leonardo DiCaprio?

Follow-up: Who's your biggest celebrity crush?

YOU MUST CHOOSE!

Would you rather...

constantly be followed by Simon Cowell judging your life

OR

by Randy Jackson yelling, "Yeah, dawg!"?

Would you rather...

fall as you walk up to accept an Oscar

OR

be caught lip-synching a performance at the Grammys?

YOU MUST CHOOSE!

Would you rather...

be a backup dancer for Justin Timberlake

OR

a backup singer for Rihanna?

Would you rather...

your dad be Billy Ray Cyrus

OR

Hulk Hogan?

YOU MUST CHOOSE!

Would you rather...

have Adele's voice

OR

Rihanna's dance moves?

Would you rather...

have a reality show based on your life

OR

be tracked and followed by the paparazzi?

YOU MUST CHOOSE!

Would you rather...

be the personal assistant to Mariah Carey

OR

Beyoncé?

YOU MUST CHOOSE!

Would you rather...

not wash your hair for a month to meet Zac Efron

OR

eat dog food for a week to meet Chace Crawford?

Would you rather...

have a celebrity alter ego (like Miley Cyrus's Hannah Montana)

OR

a superhero alter ego (like Bruce Wayne's Batman)?

YOU MUST CHOOSE!

Would you rather...

star in a movie with Taylor Lautner

OR

record a duet with Akon on his next album?

Would you rather...

your life coach be Barack Obama

OR

Bono?

YOU MUST CHOOSE!

Would you rather...

be a Justice model

OR

shop free at Justice for life?

Would you rather...

be a sister to the Jonas Brothers

OR

to the Olsen twins?

YOU MUST CHOOSE!

Would you rather...

be forced to watch 24 straight hours of CNN

OR

The Weather Channel?

YOU MUST CHOOSE!

Would you rather...

have Ashley Tisdale's arms

OR

Anne Hathaway's legs?

YOU MUST CHOOSE!

Would you rather...

your parents have named you Apple

OR

Suri?

Follow-up: What's the weirdest name you'd give a kid?

YOU MUST CHOOSE!

Would you rather...

have to clean Lindsay Lohan's house after a party

OR

organize Paris Hilton's entire closet?

YOU MUST CHOOSE!

Would you rather...

star in your high school play opposite Jack Black

OR

sing a duet in your high school talent show with John Mayer?

YOU MUST CHOOSE!

Would you rather...

be married to Gavin Rossdale

OR

Chris Martin?

YOU MUST CHOOSE!

Would you rather...

be serenaded by Jesse McCartney

OR

Jason Mraz?

YOU MUST CHOOSE!

Would you rather...

be a contestant on American Idol

OR

Minute to Win It?

Follow-up: On what show would you most want to be a contestant?

YOU MUST CHOOSE!

Would you rather...

be an actress in the next Harry Potter movie

OR

the next *Twilight* movie?

YOU MUST CHOOSE!

Would you rather...

provide a voice for a new character on *The Simpsons*

OR

The Fairly Odd Parents?

YOU MUST CHOOSE!

Who would you your substitute teacher be...

Steve Carrell **OR** Duane "The Rock" Johnson?

Lucas Grabeel **OR** Corbin Bleu?

Joe Jonas **OR** Nick Jonas **OR** Kevin Jonas?

YOU MUST CHOOSE!

Which celeb perk would you rather have:

personal hair and make-up artists

OR

a personal shopper?

Follow-up: What do you think would be the coolest perk to being a celebrity?

YOU MUST CHOOSE!

Thumbs Up, Thumbs Down

Circle the thumb that most reflects your feelings for each item below:

👍 ✊ 👎 Glee

👍 ✊ 👎 Ruby & the Rockits

👍 ✊ 👎 Wizards of Waverly Place

👍 ✊ 👎 Enchanted

👍 ✊ 👎 pigtails

👍 ✊ 👎 Tom Felton (Draco Malfoy)

👍 ✊ 👎 Uggs

👍 ✊ 👎 Katy Perry

👍 ✊ 👎 MTV

👍 ✊ 👎 Anklets

👍 ✊ 👎 Lady Gaga

👍 ✊ 👎 Piercings

CHAPTER

School

School is all about answering questions. Questions on tests, questions where you're called on in class, questions about why you are forced to learn a bunch of stupid useless junk—it never seems to end. Fortunately for you, here are some questions where there are no wrong answers.

Would you rather...

be able to silence your teacher's voice at will

OR

never have to take a math class again?

Would you rather...

have your principal be Ben Stiller

OR

Jim Carrey?

Follow-up: What other star would you want as a principal?

YOU MUST CHOOSE!

Would you rather...

take a "class" on reading celebrity gossip blogs

OR

critiquing Oscar dresses?

Follow-up: If you could take a class on anything, what would it be?

YOU MUST CHOOSE!

Would you rather...

have to go to school in a neon green wardrobe

OR

with your hair cut in the style of a mullet?

YOU MUST CHOOSE!

Would you rather...

learn Spanish in a study-abroad program in Spain

OR

from private tutoring lessons with
Wilmer Valderrama?

Would you rather...

get assigned a seat next to all the most popular
kids in school

OR

be able to turn any grade into an "A" just by blinking?

YOU MUST CHOOSE!

Would you rather...

have to be accompanied to class by your mom

OR

your brother/sister?

Would you rather...

go to a school where your teachers direct
all questions in class to only you

OR

where you're given twice as much homework
as the other students get?

YOU MUST CHOOSE!

Would you rather...

get paired on a class project with the most annoying kid in school

OR

your worst enemy?

YOU MUST CHOOSE!

Would you rather...

drop your lunch tray in the cafeteria

OR

fart in class?

Would you rather...

have a teacher that teaches in rap

OR

Pig Latin?

Things to think about: Which of your teachers would you most like to see rap?

YOU MUST CHOOSE!

Would you rather...

be voted "most likely to succeed"

OR

"most popular"?

Follow-up: What "most/best" award would you like to win?

YOU MUST CHOOSE!

Would you rather...

have pencils that can write in any font

OR

be able to erase a chalkboard just by thinking really hard about it?

Would you rather...

be the smartest girl in class

OR

the best dresser?

YOU MUST CHOOSE!

Would you rather...

your gym teacher be LeBron James

OR

your music teacher be Justin Timberlake?

YOU MUST CHOOSE!

Would you rather...

be yearbook editor

OR

band leader?

Would you rather...

never have to study and still ace your classes

OR

never have to put in any effort and still
look great?

YOU MUST CHOOSE!

Would you rather...

go to a school where you break out into musical numbers like in *High School Musical*

OR

that is full of magic like Hogwarts?

Third option: Forks High School (from *Twilight*)?

YOU MUST CHOOSE!

Would you...

cheat on a test if you knew no one would find out?

sign up for a class project with your crush if you had to do his share of the work?

get rid of the first letter of your name to raise every grade on your report card?

YOU MUST CHOOSE!

Would you rather...

go to a school dance in a sweat suit

OR

go to a school dance with your little brother?

YOU MUST CHOOSE!

Would you rather...

attend an all-girls school

OR

a boarding school 300 miles from home?

Would you rather...

write "I will not talk in class" 500 times on the blackboard

OR

wear duct tape over your mouth all day?

YOU MUST CHOOSE!

Would you rather...

only be allowed to communicate via written notes

OR

by texting?

YOU MUST CHOOSE!

Would you rather...

be fined 50 dollars every time you swear

OR

be fined 50 dollars every time you say "like"
("I was like, then she was like..." etc.)?

YOU MUST CHOOSE!

Would you rather...

eat cafeteria food for dinner every night

OR

week-old bagels for breakfast every morning?

YOU MUST CHOOSE!

Would you rather...

spill your backpack in class and have your private notes from your friends spill out

OR

walk around all day with your fly down?

Follow-up: What's the most embarrassing thing you've done around a boy you like?

YOU MUST CHOOSE!

Would you rather your teachers be...

clowns **OR** mimes?

romance novelists **OR** dog trainers?

professional wrestlers **OR** weathermen?

YOU MUST CHOOSE!

Would you rather...

your school mascot be a Chihuahua **OR** a meerkat?

a porcupine **OR** a salmon?

a toaster oven **OR** a ham and cheese sandwich?

YOU MUST CHOOSE!

Would you rather...

be the star of the basketball team

OR

the glee club?

YOU MUST CHOOSE!

Would you rather...

read your text messages aloud in class

OR

read your diary aloud in class?

YOU MUST CHOOSE!

Would you rather...

get to school via horse-drawn carriage

OR

helicopter?

YOU MUST CHOOSE!

Would you rather...

your gym uniform be a wool sweater

OR

a footie pajamas?

YOU MUST CHOOSE!

Would you rather...

go to school seven days a week for two hours a day

OR

two days a week for twelve hours a day?

YOU MUST CHOOSE!

CHAPTER

Friends, Frenemies and BFFs

They say you can judge a girl by the friends she keeps, but who your friends are only tells half the story. Would you throw your BFF under the bus for a boy? Do you truly prize loyalty above all else? It's time to find out where you and your best friends really stand.

Would you rather...

be BFFs with Gabriella Montez

OR

Sharpay Evans?

Follow-up: What fictional character do you think would make the best BFF?

YOU MUST CHOOSE!

Would you rather...

have a friend who always borrows money

OR

who always borrows your clothes, then "forgets" to return them?

YOU MUST CHOOSE!

Would you rather...

your BFF be smarter than you

OR

prettier than you?

YOU MUST CHOOSE!

Would you rather...

have to compete against your BFF for the star spot on the girls' basketball team

OR

have to compete against her for your mutual crush's affection?

YOU MUST CHOOSE!

Would you rather...

get to spend a day looking exactly like your BFF

OR

looking exactly like your worst enemy?

Things to think about: Helping out your best friend. Getting even with your worst enemy.

YOU MUST CHOOSE!

Would you rather...

be equipped with a Friend Lie Detector

OR

a Boy Lie Detector?

YOU MUST CHOOSE!

Would you rather...

a frenemy write an embarrassing blog post about you

OR

post embarrassing pictures of you online?

Would you rather...

have ten casual friends

OR

one best friend?

YOU MUST CHOOSE!

Would you rather...

not be able to keep a secret

OR

not be able to tell a lie?

YOU MUST CHOOSE!

Which friend set would you rather be in?

Brains **OR** Jocks?

Band **OR** Skaters?

Preppy **OR** Punk?

YOU MUST CHOOSE!

Would you rather...

have a friend tell you when someone was spreading lies about you

OR

not tell you when someone was spreading lies about you?

YOU MUST CHOOSE!

Would you rather...

have your friends and your IM conversations broadcast on TV

OR

have a really powerful microphone broadcast your conversations all day?

YOU MUST CHOOSE!

At a friend's sleepover, would you rather. . .

drool in your sleep

OR

fart in your sleep?

YOU MUST CHOOSE!

Would you rather...

have a friend who talked obsessively about her crush (who you can't stand)

OR

who talked obsessively about physics?

YOU MUST CHOOSE!

Would you rather...

your frenemy get an A in every class

OR

your frenemy get a whole closet of cool new clothes?

YOU MUST CHOOSE!

Would you rather...

stay in detention for a friend

OR

tell her parents that she got detention?

Would you rather...

borrow your best friend's bike and put a small scratch on it

OR

borrow her expensive new dress and rip it?

YOU MUST CHOOSE!

What's your most valued characteristic in a BFF?

loyalty **OR** honesty?

humor **OR** looks?

social status **OR** money?

YOU MUST CHOOSE!

Would you rather...

not have a single class with your BFF

OR

sit by _____ in every class?
<small>(insert name of girl you can't stand)</small>

YOU MUST CHOOSE!

Would you rather...

be the last of your friends to have her braces removed

OR

the last to pass her driver's test?

YOU MUST CHOOSE!

Would you rather...

a friend copy everything you do (clothes, hair, etc.)

OR

make fun of everything you do?

YOU MUST CHOOSE!

Would you rather...

have a friend who always talked in a robot voice

OR

in IM-speak ("btw," "lol," etc.)?

YOU MUST CHOOSE!

Would you rather...

have a friend who has the Princess Leia 'ear muffs' hairdo

OR

permanent bad breath?

YOU MUST CHOOSE!

Which celebrities would you rather be BFFs with?

Katy Perry **OR** Taylor Swift?

Tyra Banks **OR** Paris Hilton?

Anne Hathaway **OR** Emmy Rossum?

YOU MUST CHOOSE!

Would you rather...

be able to magically fit into any friend's outfits

OR

be able to inflict spontaneous breakouts on girls you don't like?

YOU MUST CHOOSE!

Would you rather...

always know when people were gossiping about you

OR

only be able to hear compliments?

YOU MUST CHOOSE!

105

For the questions below, choose option a, b or c

1. My ideal BFF is:

   a. smart

   b. hilarious

   c. pretty

2. If my BFF and I saw an outfit we both liked in a store, I would:

   a. Let her buy it.

   b. Suggest we both buy it and wear it on the same day as BFFs.

   c. Tell her it's not her style...and then go back and buy it later for yourself.

3. My friends love me most because:

a. I'm loyal.

b. I'm a lot of fun.

c. I'm super cute.

4. The most embarrassing thing my BFF has witnessed is:

a. Me crying hysterically over a movie.

b. Me farting really loudly.

c. Me in clothes my grandma picked out.

5. The most annoying thing about being my friend is:

a. I talk too much.

b. I really like being right.

c. Please—I'm not annoying, you are.

6. The celebrity I'd probably be friends with is:

a. Jennifer Aniston

b. Jessica Simpson

c. Beyoncé

7. My friends make fun of me because:

   a. I'm a bookworm.

   b. I'm hopeless around guys.

   c. My clothes are too tight.

8. I'm really good at:

   a. Cheering up friends when they're upset.

   b. Giving solid advice.

   c. Everything.

9. I get mad when:

   a. A friend talks behind my back.

   b. My friends get together without me.

   c. A friend looks better than I do.

10. I can't deal with a friend who's not:

   a. trustworthy

   b. fun-loving

   c. popular

Mostly A's: We'd tell you all our BFF-worthy secrets.

Mostly B's: We'd definitely hang out with you.

Mostly C's: We'd rather compete to be Paris Hilton's bestie, thanks.

Would you rather...

beat out your friend to get the lead
in the school play

OR

purposefully flub your audition so she'd get
the part?

Would you rather...

take your BFFs on a free beach vacation

OR

get a free shopping spree?

YOU MUST CHOOSE!

Would you...

tell your BFF's biggest secret in exchange for full college tuition?

not watch television for a week to help a friend study for an English test?

skip your BFF's surprise birthday party to interview Zac Efron on TV?

YOU MUST CHOOSE!

Would you rather...

permanently trade houses with your BFF

OR

siblings?

YOU MUST CHOOSE!

Would you rather...

have to sit next to _____ at school
(insert worst enemy)
for an entire year

OR

only be able to ask _____
(insert least favorite teacher)
for help with schoolwork?

YOU MUST CHOOSE!

CHAPTER

Would You?

Sometimes, simple "yes or no" questions are the hardest. Case in point: this chapter. The questions only require a one word answer, but getting to the answer is the hard part. Should you?... Could you?... Would you?

Would you...

wear your grandma's clothes to get an extra $50 per week allowance?

What would you do for $1,000?

go to school dressed as Ronald McDonald?

ignore your BFF for a week?

give all your clothes away?

YOU MUST CHOOSE!

Would you...

eat nothing but tofu for lunch if you could have whatever you wanted for dinner?

Would you...

run across the football field during halftime wearing a bunny costume for a $10,000 shopping spree?

YOU MUST CHOOSE!

Would you...

spend two weeks locked in a room with you worst enemy to appear on the cover of *Seventeen* Magazine?

YOU MUST CHOOSE!

Would you...

dye your hair green for a year for a computer and cell phone of your choice?

Would you...

give up text messaging for a year for a free trip to Paris?

Would you...

give up texting and email for the rest of your life to have a private jet?

YOU MUST CHOOSE!

Would you...

join a study group with the most annoying kids in your school for two weeks to get to make a music video with Jesse McCartney?

How about...

David Archuleta?

Justin Bieber?

The Jonas Brothers?

YOU MUST CHOOSE!

Would you...

eat a plate of deep-fried ants to be the star of a new Disney Channel show?

How about...

wearing the same outfit you are currently wearing every day for the next 3 months?

repeating an entire year of school?

shave your head and always wear different wigs?

YOU MUST CHOOSE!

Would you...

wear diapers outside your jeans for a month to grow three inches taller?

YOU MUST CHOOSE!

Would you...

pay $1,000 for the ability to memorize everything you ever read?

Follow-up: Would you want that same ability if it meant your hair would turn purple to have that power (you wouldn't need to pay the $1,000 though)?

YOU MUST CHOOSE!

Would you...

take your little brother with you everywhere if your parents gave you a $100/week allowance?

Would you...

eat a brownie dirt cup with real earthworms to get four front-row tickets for a Miley Cyrus concert?

YOU MUST CHOOSE!

Would you...

ever lie to your parents about where you were going to sneak out with your BFF?

YOU MUST CHOOSE!

Would you...

chug a gallon of milk in a minute for a lifetime supply of Starbucks?

Would you...

befriend the nerdiest kid in school if he or she would help you get better grades in every one of your classes?

YOU MUST CHOOSE!

Would you...

rat out your BFF if she did something for which you were getting blamed?

Follow-up: Would you 'fess up if she were taking the rap for you?

YOU MUST CHOOSE!

Would you...

eat a large bowl of gravy for dinner for 30 nights to be sung to on stage by Justin Timberlake?

How about...

hot sauce?

butter?

lard?

YOU MUST CHOOSE!

Would you...

want your parents to go on *What Not to Wear*?

Would you...

shower in sewer water for an hour to get to co-host *American Idol* with Ryan Seacrest for one week?

YOU MUST CHOOSE!

Would you...

use only clown makeup if doing so would mean you'd never get a zit again?

Would you...

get a permanent bright orange spray tan if you'd also get your hair to look exactly the way you'd like it to?

YOU MUST CHOOSE!

Would you...

let your parents respond to all of your texts on your behalf if they'd pay your cell phone bills for life?

YOU MUST CHOOSE!

Would you...

never miss a day of school for three years to be able to present the Best Male Singer award at next year's *Nickelodeon Kids' Choice Awards*?

YOU MUST CHOOSE!

Would you...

study 5 hours a day for a test if an "A" would get you a full college scholarship?

How about if you had...

> a 20% chance of passing?

> a 50% chance?

> a 75% chance?

YOU MUST CHOOSE!

Would you...

keep your BFF's biggest secret in the world if you were offered $10 million to tell?

YOU MUST CHOOSE!

Would you...

want the power to be invisible if every time you disappeared and reappeared you had a new pimple that would last at least a week?

YOU MUST CHOOSE!

Thumbs Up, Thumbs Down

Circle the thumb that most reflects your feelings for each item below:

👍 👎 👎 Terrycloth pants   👍 👎 👎 NASCAR

👍 👎 👎 Simon Cowell

👍 👎 👎 John Mayer

👍 👎 👎 Dramatic
chipmunk
(on YouTube)

👍 👎 👎 Raven-Symoné

👍 👎 👎 Leggings

👍 👎 👎 Britney Spears

👍 👎 👎 Commercials

👍 👎 👎 Twilight

👍 👎 👎 Bottled water

👍 👎 👎 Abrevs

CHAPTER

Getting personal

It's time to get personal! Challenge your friends with these personalized puzzlers involving people you know and love (and hate.)

Would you rather...

spend 5 hours in a car with _____
(insert incredibly annoying acquaintance)

OR

be stuck in an elevator for 10 hours with

_____ ?
(insert acquaintance with terrible hygiene)

Would you rather...

make out with _____ and _____ as
(insert teacher)   (insert teacher)
your parents

OR

have your parents as teachers ?

Things to think about: goofing off, nightly dinners, who's more strict?

YOU MUST CHOOSE!

Would you rather...

have a ketchup stain on your blouse in front of

_____
(insert crush's name)

OR

get caught passing notes to a friend in

_____ 's classroom?
(insert teacher's name)

Would you rather...

appear as _____ in all
(insert cartoon character)
photographs

OR

_____
(insert person)

sound like   on all
recordings?

YOU MUST CHOOSE!

Would you rather...

have the hair of _____
(insert schoolmate with bad hair)

OR

wear the same clothes as _____ ?
(insert schoolmate with awful style)

Would you rather...

get into an argument with _____
(insert girl friend)

OR

get so angry you stop talking to _____ ?
(insert girl friend)

YOU MUST CHOOSE!

Would you rather...

share a bedroom with_____
(insert messiest friend)

OR

share clothes with _____ ?
(insert worst-dressed friend)

YOU MUST CHOOSE!

Would you rather...

read _____ for 5 hours
(insert boring textbook)

OR

watch _____ for 10 hours?
(insert mindless reality TV show)

Would you rather...

listen to every song on _____ 's iPod
(insert lame acquaintance)

OR

every song by _____ ?
(insert bad band)

YOU MUST CHOOSE!

Would you rather...

be a taste-tester for _____
(insert favorite restaurant)

OR

a fashion-tester for _____ ?
(insert favorite brand)

YOU MUST CHOOSE!

Would you rather...

be able to get a higher grade than _____
(insert smartest classmate)

OR

be considered better looking than _____ ?
(insert best-looking classmate)

Would you rather...

be able to magically redecorate your _____
(insert room of your house)

OR

move the house you have to _____ ?
(insert city)

YOU MUST CHOOSE!

Would you rather...

wear 10 pounds of _____
(insert accessory)

OR

have to go without _____ ?
(insert article of clothing)

YOU MUST CHOOSE!

Would you rather...

win a free vacation to _____
(insert location)

OR

never have to pay for _____ again?
(insert noun)

Would you rather...

share your e-mails with _____
(insert family member)

OR

share your BFF with _____ ?
(insert worst enemy)

YOU MUST CHOOSE!

Would you rather...

arrive at school in a _____
(insert emergency vehicle)

OR

on a _____?
(insert animal)

YOU MUST CHOOSE!

Would you rather...

instantly be able to speak perfect _____
(insert foreign language)

OR

spend a month in _____ ?
(insert foreign country)

YOU MUST CHOOSE!

Would you rather...

wash your hair with_____
(insert liquid)

OR

cut your nails with _____?
(insert sharp object)

YOU MUST CHOOSE!

Insert three female celebrities:

_____

_____

_____

Who would you rather...

Go shopping with?

Look like?

Get into a fight with?

YOU MUST CHOOSE!

Insert three male celebrities:

_____

_____

_____

Who would you rather...

have at your next birthday party?

sit next to on an airplane?

give you a shout-out during
his next interview?

YOU MUST CHOOSE!

Would you rather...

star on _____

(insert TV show)

OR

live next door to _____ ?

(insert celebrity)

Would you rather...

have _____

(insert magical power)

OR

_____ ?

(insert dollar amount)

YOU MUST CHOOSE!

Would you rather...

lose your mom's favorite _____
(insert jewelry)

OR

ruin your dad's _____ ?
(insert favorite thing)

YOU MUST CHOOSE!

Would you give up _____
(insert prized possession)

for...

a new car?

a trip to Italy?

perfect hair?

YOU MUST CHOOSE!

Would you rather...

eat only _____
(insert candy)

OR

drink only _____ ?
(insert beverage)

Would you rather...

go back to age _____
(insert younger age)

OR

skip ahead to age _____ ?
(insert older age)

YOU MUST CHOOSE!

Would you rather...

be handcuffed to _____ for a week
(insert annoying acquaintance)

OR

not be able to talk to _____ for a month?
(insert good friend)

Would you rather...

have a potion that repelled _____
(insert adjective)
classmates

OR

a potion that attracted _____
(insert adjective)
classmates?

YOU MUST CHOOSE!

Would you rather...

be able to _____
(insert talent)

OR

_____ ?
(insert superhero power)

YOU MUST CHOOSE!

159

Would you rather...

smell like _____ no matter how much you
(insert foul odor)
showered

OR

have a permanent zit on your _____ ?
(insert body part/facial feature)

Would you rather...

ride to school in a bus with seats
made of _____
(insert hard object)

OR

have to share a bus seat with _____ ?
(insert unappealing person)

YOU MUST CHOOSE!

Would you rather...

rip your _____ in the middle of class
(insert article of clothing)

OR

fall asleep in class and _____
(insert verb)
in your sleep?

YOU MUST CHOOSE!

Would you rather...

have to tell on _____ for breaking
(insert person)
school rules

OR

have to tell the story of _____
(insert embarrassing moment)
in front of the whole school?

Would you rather...

have a BFF who only wore _____
(insert bad fashion choice)

OR

who was terrible at _____?
(insert activity)

YOU MUST CHOOSE!

Would you rather...

be BFF with _____
(insert male celebrity)

OR

look like _____ ?
(insert female celebrity)

YOU MUST CHOOSE!

Would you rather...

grow so tall that you are _____ inches taller
(insert number)
than the tallest girl at your school

OR

your nose grow_____?
(insert length)

YOU MUST CHOOSE!

Instead of detention, would you rather your punishment be...

spending a week with _____
(insert obnoxious classmate)

OR

joining a study group with_____ ?
(insert unattractive guy)

YOU MUST CHOOSE!

CHAPTER

Random Play

You've handled all the tough questions and quandaries so far. But now, you have no idea what to expect....

Would you rather...

be able to burp the alphabet

OR

play "Happy Birthday" with your armpit?

Would you rather...

speak in tongues when you're nervous

OR

projectile vomit?

YOU MUST CHOOSE!

Would you rather...

have a giant wardrobe

OR

a giant allowance?

YOU MUST CHOOSE!

Would you rather...

give up your cell phone

OR

your computer?

YOU MUST CHOOSE!

Would you rather...

have glue-tipped fingers

OR

pogo-stick feet?

YOU MUST CHOOSE!

Would you rather...

brush your teeth with dishwashing liquid

OR

wash your hair with laundry detergent?

Would you rather...

not be allowed to use your hands when you eat

OR

not be allowed to sleep lying down?

YOU MUST CHOOSE!

Would you rather...

have superhuman hearing

OR

superhuman vision?

YOU MUST CHOOSE!

Would you rather...

share bunk beds with your brattiest sibling

OR

share a bathroom with every one of your cousins?

Would you rather...

face Simon on *American Idol*

OR

break your ankle on *Dancing with the Stars*?

YOU MUST CHOOSE!

What would you do to get to meet Robert Pattinson?

Go without sleep for three days?

Make monkey noises instead of speaking for a week?

Give up a month's allowance?

YOU MUST CHOOSE!

Would you rather...

have everything you do automatically Twittered

OR

automatically texted to your parents' cell phones?

Would you rather...

eat a peanut-butter-and-chicken-liver sandwich

OR

drink a raw-egg-and-hot-sauce milkshake?

Follow-up: What's the grossest thing you ever consumed?

YOU MUST CHOOSE!

Would you rather...

win $1 million

OR

get music lessons for a month with
the Jonas Brothers?

YOU MUST CHOOSE!

Would you rather...

wear garlic-scented perfume

OR

mushroom-flavored lip gloss?

Would you rather...

be able to "pause" the world whenever you wanted

OR

be able to have the world "rewind" when you make a mistake?

YOU MUST CHOOSE!

Would you rather...

have rapidly growing leg hair

OR

hair growing out of your ears?

YOU MUST CHOOSE!

Would you rather...

get locked in the mall after closing time

OR

be stuck on the ferris wheel at an amusement park after closing time?

YOU MUST CHOOSE!

Would you rather...

your crush study with you for a big test

OR

be able to learn everything just by sleeping with the textbook under your pillow?

YOU MUST CHOOSE!

Would you rather...

wake up each day with a new hair color and style

OR

a new last name?

Would you rather...

always get "A"'s without ever having to study

OR

have a great body without ever having to diet?

YOU MUST CHOOSE!

Would you rather...

have a fight with your BFF in the hallway between classes

OR

via text message?

YOU MUST CHOOSE!

About the Author

Courtney Balestier is a writer and editor thrilled to finally have a shame-free outlet for her *Gossip Girl* obsessions. When she's not wondering how Blair Waldorf's headband stays in place or why Chuck Bass speaks in a permanent whisper, Courtney can be found writing, talking or thinking about food and music, though not necessarily together. (Luckily, she has found publications willing to publish her work that don't frown upon such behavior.) Courtney lives in Brooklyn, by way of Morgantown, West Virginia.

Are you ready for more
Would You Rather...?

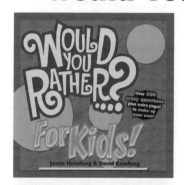